Raspberry Pi

The complete guide to Raspberry Pi for beginners, including projects, tips, tricks, and programming

Table of Contents

Introduction

Thank you for taking the time to pick up this book about Raspberry Pi!

This book serves as a beginner's guide to the world of Raspberry Pi, the different models, how to use them, and what their capabilities are.

In the following chapters, you will discover the power of the Raspberry Pi microcomputer, which model is the right one for you, how to set up your Pi for use, and how to get started on your very first Raspberry Pi project!

You will discover the different programming languages that can be used on the Pi, and which ones are best for you to start with. Also included are some fun and simple projects that you can try, that are perfect for the beginner Pi user!

Once again, thanks for choosing this book, I hope you find it to be helpful.

Chapter 1: Raspberry Pi 101

Simply put, the Raspberry Pi is a computer that is merely the size of a credit card that can plug into your television. It is a device that is capable of many of the same basic processing tasks as a laptop or desktop computer, and it can do things like access and edit spreadsheets, compute basic word processing, browse the internet, and house games the owner can play. It also has the capability to play high-definition video as well as store an entire audio library.

When the Raspberry Pi first came into being, the sole purpose of the device was to create a learning tool that could be distributed to third-world developing countries in order to expose children, especially young girls, to the entire world of computer science and programming. The Raspberry Pi was going to be an affordable device centered completely around teaching the world of programming so children in these countries had a chance to afford themselves a better life.

The Raspberry Pi device can be easily purchased from many main distributors that the Raspberry Pi Foundation has certified. Premier Farnell/Element14 as well as RS Components/Allied Electronics are just two of many distributors set around the globe that are legally allowed to distribute Raspberry Pi devices with specific guarantees set by the Foundation itself. There are also several resellers of the Raspberry Pi device you can access both online as well as in brick-and-mortar stores.

When you purchase a Raspberry Pi device, you simply get the board itself. A power supply and an SD card are going to be necessary in order to power your Raspberry Pi, but unless you purchase a kit you are going to have to purchase them separately. You can also buy preloaded SD cards that come with already-installed operating systems that will help diminish the time it takes for you to set up your Raspberry Pi to work the way you wish. However, you need to make sure you purchase these preloaded SD cards only from licensed distributors instead of from third-party distributors like eBay. The reason being is the fact that their software is updated regularly, so these cards that are sold by all of these third parties can become outdated incredibly quickly, resulting in a corrupted or mute piece of technology.

The Raspberry Pi was developed in the United Kingdom by the pre-established Raspberry Pi Foundation. While it was supposed to teach the basics of computer science and programming to various schools in the developing world, the original model became far more popular than they could have ever anticipated. The device, in its original generation, sold outside of its original target market and became incredibly popular in other areas such as robotics. To date, over 15 million Raspberry Pi devices have been sold worldwide, and they have seen implementations from self-flying drones all the way to being utilized in manufacturing plants as durable, long-lasting computers.

There have been many generations of the Raspberry Pi device, but the first generation was released in February 2012. Since then, every major update the Raspberry Pi device has had has resulted in another model that has been substantially more popular than the last. What started out as basic updates to a credit-card sized computer, turned into trying to make this credit card-sized computer function the same as a full-sized computer. As the Foundation and the developers began to improve the product, they started to add capabilities like wireless internet access, Ethernet ports, and Bluetooth connectivity.

All of the Raspberry Pi models feature an SoC, which is a Broadcom system-on-a-chip. This SoC includes an ARM central processing unit that is compatible with the on-chip graphics processing unit, and each time a new iteration of the Raspberry Pi is created, these common systems are updated. Most of the boards also have a tailored number of USB slots, ranging from one slot to four. They also house composite video output as well as HDMI, and a 3.5 mm phone jack for audio.

And, as if that is not enough, the Raspberry Pi comes with its own Debian-based operating system, entitled Raspbian. Do not be alarmed, however, because this is not the only operating system that can run on the device itself. There are many iterations of Windows 10, Ubuntu, and many other popular operating systems that can easily be downloaded onto the Raspberry Pi in order to customize the experience you have with your device.

However, one of the greatest things about the Raspberry Pi is that it supports peripheral devices. This does not simply stop at a keyboard, mouse, and monitor, but it also means the Raspberry Pi can be utilized in several at-home projects, from creating your own e-book library and media entertainment center, all the way to setting up your own home surveillance system.

No matter the generation of the Raspberry Pi, they all come with the same basic parts found in a laptop or desktop computer. There is a processor, which is the broadcom SoC mentioned earlier, and it is similar to the chips that were used in the first modern generations of smartphones. While different generations have different processing power, they all has some sort of processor in order to make the Pi device work. In some versions, like the first-generation Raspberry Pi, the processor is a little chip that is stacked underneath the RAM chip, which can make it hard to find if you are trying to update it or switch it out.

As the Raspberry Pi developed, the strength and performance of the processor improved. The Raspberry Pi 3 houses a quad-core Cortex-A53 processor, and it has been tested and proven to have ten times the performance speed and accuracy of the first-generation Raspberry Pi. Not only that, but the processor of the Raspberry Pi 3 is 80% faster than its previous generation, which is a massive update that was taken on by the Foundation.

The Raspberry Pi also comes with overclocking capabilities. Overclocking is simply the ability to push a computer's components higher and faster than the manufacturer's guidelines. Most of the Raspberry Pi's onboard chips can be overclocked anywhere between 800 and 1000 MHz, and this is a bonus for individuals who are purchasing the Raspberry Pi for the sole purpose of using it as a computer replacement. The truth of the matter is that size does matter when it comes to some technological components, so the idea of overclocking allows the owner of the Raspberry Pi to enhance the speed and processing capability of their Raspberry Pi device in an attempt to match that of a laptop or desktop computer.

The owner just has to make sure there is a way to cool the Raspberry Pi down whenever it is being overclocked, otherwise the overheating can do a lot of damage to your device.

The Raspberry Pi does have built-in protection mechanisms when it is being overclocked, however. If any of the chips on the Pi reach 185 degrees Fahrenheit, the Raspberry Pi will automatically shut itself down. It is possible to override these automatic over-voltage settings, but it will void your warranty with the store you purchased it at, and it's likely to do damage.

Then, there is the RAM. This is the memory of the computer, and this is one of the most highly-developed areas in all of the generations of the Raspberry Pi. In the beginning, only 128 MB was allocated by default to the memory of the Raspberry Pi. This meant the earlier models could either run a 1080p video decoding or a simple 3D image, but they could not run both of them together. As the Raspberry Pi models progressed, however, that memory increased. The Raspberry Pi 3, one of the most recent generations of the device, has one gigabyte of RAM. They worked hard in order to incorporate as much memory as possible into this little device because they knew that memory storage was going to be one of the things that would make or break their updated devices on the market. They listened to complaints and needs in other markets outside of their target market, and one of those consistent complaints was that the downside to the Raspberry Pi in general was its lack of memory storage. Many people, especially in the robotics community, complained that the memory storage alone is what would cause the Raspberry Pi to soon lag behind other microcomputers.

Then, there is the networking aspect of the Raspberry Pi. The very first generations had no wireless internet or Ethernet circuitry, which meant they had to utilize an external user supplied USB Ethernet, or wireless internet adapter. However, one of the big changes they made with the Raspberry Pi Model B and B+ was to install an onboard Ethernet port in order to gain access to the internet without utilizing a USB Ethernet adapter. Then, with the development of the Raspberry Pi 3 and the

Raspberry Pi Zero W came the ability to utilize wireless internet access. To date, it is the most popular update they have made with the Raspberry Pi, and it is what made the Raspberry Pi 3 so lusted after by the technology industry.

The good thing about the Raspberry Pi, however, is that no matter how many times it is updated, your peripherals do not have to update with it. You can use any generic USB keyboard and mouse in order to operate your Raspberry Pi, and this can greatly cut the cost of the overall purchase. Even though the newer generations of the Pi device can give better graphics on a high-end monitor, you do not have to use a high-end monitor. It is possible to scale down the resolution and the input/output of the video components to work with an older monitor or television, which is why the Raspberry Pi 3 is the most versatile of all the Pi generations.

Then, there is the video aspect of the Raspberry Pi. This is where the graphics of the device come into play, and the most recent generations can emit standard television resolutions such as HD and Full HD. Do not think, however, that just because the Raspberry Pi has the capability of playing these videos that it can also decode them, because that is not always the case. Although the Raspberry Pi 3 has the ability to play some of the highest definition videos on the market, it does not have H.265 decoding software, even though its CPU is more powerful than its predecessors.

The last component that comes equipped in some form on all the Raspberry Pi devices is a real-time clock. While it does not have an automatically-updated clock built into the device, there is a program that runs naturally on the Pi device that can retrieve the time and date from a network time server, or it can be retrieved by simple user input at the time of boot up. In order to help keep some sort of consistency for the built-in file system on the Raspberry Pi device, it does automatically save the time and date it has installed upon the device's shut down, and it reinstalls that same time and date on boot up in order to help the owner of the device toggle the date and time to its necessary numbers.

But even though all Raspberry Pi generations have the same basic features, these features take on different, and usually larger, components as the Raspberry Pi device has evolved through its iterations. Understanding these differences is going to help you pick the Pi device that will be right for you and the purpose you wish to utilize it for, and knowing these specs can sometimes help you to choose which project you will take on simply based upon the Raspberry Pi generation you feel most comfortable working with.

Chapter 2: The Different Models & Their Features

The models of the Raspberry Pi currently available on the distributing market are the Raspberry Pi 2 Model B, the Raspberry Pi 3 Model B, the Raspberry Pi Zero, the Raspberry Pi Zero W, the Raspberry Pi 1 Model A+, and the Raspberry Pi 1 Model B+. Each of these iterations of the Raspberry Pi come with different specs that enable you to do different things, which is why understanding their differences is to vital. The Raspberry Pi model A+ has a BCM2835 SoC, a processing speed of 700 MHz, 512 MB of RAM, one USB port, and no onboard Ethernet port or wireless and/or Bluetooth capabilities. This means you will need extra peripherals outside of a monitor, keyboard, and mouse in order to access the internet in order to attempt many at-home projects that are popular in the Raspberry Pi world.

However, they changed two things with the Raspberry Pi Model B+: they added three more USB ports and they made the internet accessible via an onboard Ethernet port. This made the Raspberry Pi more accessible in the world of robotics, as well as in the realm of setting up and customizing cheap, personal, individual computers for those who simply wanted a cheaper alternative to desktop and laptop computers.

The Raspberry Pi Model B generation comes with two different types of onboard SoCs: You can get it with the BCM2836 or the BCM2837. It also has a higher processing speed of 900 MHz, has 1GB of RAM memory, four USB ports, and comes with an onboard Ethernet input slot. However, this generation does not have wireless or Bluetooth capabilities. This iteration of the Pi device helped the robotics community greatly with the massive uptick in available memory, and it toned down their complaints... at least momentarily. Coupling that with the four USB ports, one would assume that the technological communities that had come to rely on this device for their internals would have been happy with where the device now stood. Sales don't lie: when this generation was released, it was

8

the highest-selling generation the Foundation had seen of all its Pi devices.

But, all good things always have a downside, and this was when the technological community as a whole started to uproar again despite all the additions. They felt the Pi device, was still lagging behind the technological community by not finding a way to make the device compatible with wireless internet access. Not only that, but the robotics community underwent a major shift towards the mass utilization of Bluetooth technology, and the Foundation found that one of their biggest unintentional target markets was beginning to stray away once again from the device because of the inability to obtain wireless internet access and utilize Bluetooth technology.

So, the Foundation answered their cries for help with the Raspberry Pi 3 Model B generation. While the onboard SoC moved permanently to the BCM2837, the processing speed jumped to 1200 MHz. It still housed the one gigabyte of RAM memory, the four USB ports, and the onboard Ethernet port for internet connectivity, but now the device also had wireless internet access capabilities and allowed the use of outside Bluetooth technologies. To date, within many vast technological communities this is the highest-selling Raspberry Pi model the Foundation has created. However, the Foundation was not done there. Once the complaining about the device died down, they were able to focus on other areas the Raspberry Pi could expand into. In their eyes, they had made all of the improvements they could to the credit card-sized device that they could foresee, so they worked to create an even cheaper device that could make this technology more accessible to the masses they were not tapping into.

Even though many Raspberry Pi models are priced anywhere between $20 and $35, the Foundation outdid itself by producing the Raspberry Pi Zero and the Raspberry Pi Zero W. Both of them utilized the BCM2835 as the onboard SoC, they both had a processing speed of 1000 MHz, they both had an internal RAM memory of 512 MB, and they both had one USB port each. However, this is where their differences begin: the Raspberry Pi

Model Zero does not have an onboard Ethernet access port, wireless internet capabilities, or Bluetooth compatibility. But, the Raspberry Pi Zero W has wireless and Bluetooth capabilities, even though it does not have an onboard Ethernet access port. These versions today sell for anywhere between $5 and $10, making them the most monetarily-accessible Raspberry Pi unit on the market.

All of the Raspberry Pi models, in some form, have GPIO pins, or general purpose input/output pins. This makes other peripherals that can be utilized with the Raspberry Pi accessible, even though you might not have the onboard USB ports to plug them into. All Raspberry Pi models have some number of GPIO pins installed on the outer edges of them, but the most recent generations have been created with 40 GPIO pins for each device rendered.

However, there is one final model that has not been described that the Foundation created for one very specific purpose: it is the Raspberry Pi CM, which stands for "Compute Model," and it is intended specifically for industrial applications. In June 2014, a Polish industrial automation manufacturer ended up designing the globe's first industrial computer that was based solely on the Raspberry Pi. TECHBASE, the Polish manufacturer, called it the "ModBerry." This was a device that had numerous interfaces along with multiple digital and analog inputs and outputs. It housed CAN and economical 1-Wire buses, all of which are used in the automation industry, and the particular design the Polish manufacturing company developed enabled the Raspberry Pi to operate in it's harsh industrial environment. This is what sparked the revolutionary design of the Raspberry Pi CM model because they realized their device was no longer limited to simply science projects and in-home crafts.

So, they created the official Raspberry Pi Compute Module.

This particular Raspberry Pi device is smaller than the usual devices and it gives manufacturers a very easy and cheap way to use the entire Raspberry Pi ecosystem within their own technological devices in their warehouses. They are built to be encased in metals and plastics that can withstand the industrial environment they are being subjected to, and they have the potential to storm the manufacturing market and drastically lower the technological costs of updating systems within a warehouse.

That is not the only modern implementation of the Raspberry Pi, however, that stands outside of the realm of in-home projects. OTTO is a digital camera that was created by Next Thing Co., and it has incorporated the Raspberry Pi Compute Module into its own digital camera layout and interface. This was a project that was successfully crowd-funded by Kickstarter in May 2014, and has since taken the market by storm, utilizing the Compute Module of the Raspberry Pi at the heart of its product. Not only that, but Slice, a digital media player, also uses this Compute Module form of the Raspberry Pi at the heart of its product. It was successfully crowd-funded in August 2014 on a different Kickstarter campaign, and it was yet another avenue to catapult this device to places the Foundation never could have foreseen.

Then, the Raspberry Pi found its way into the world of space exploration. There was a project that was launched in December 2014 at an event held by the United Kingdom space agency. It was called the Astro Pi competition, and it officially opened in January 2014 to all primary and secondary school-aged children who were residents of the UK. The particular mission of this project was to deploy these computers onboard the International Space Station during astronaut Tim Peake's space exploration mission, in order to find more efficient and creative ways of transmitting data from the astronauts to their respective home bases. What happened was the winning code would be loaded to Tim Peake while he was in orbit so he could collect data that was generated on his end and send it back to Earth where it could be distributed among those who need the information the most. Information and statistics such as satellite imaging, space measurements, data fusion, spacecraft sensors, and space radiation were all relayed back via the winning code to the home base of the astronaut, and the winning team members got the classified access of seeing their code work in real-time.

The competition was an attempt to stimulate scientific and creative thinking within the Raspberry Pi realm by tapping into future generations.

Even though the Raspberry Pi device had a very small target market in the beginning, it has grown into one of the most accessible technological devices ever seen. Industries like manufacturing and space exploration have started to utilize this product to help cut costs and improve the efficiency of their products and data transmissions, and the Foundation is more popular than ever for their improvements and developments born out of listening to their customers wishes and complaints. Not only has the Raspberry Pi device sold millions upon millions of units, it has made computer science and computer programming accessible to every single person on the planet.

Whether you are a technological expert or someone who is simply wanting to find a cheaper alternative to a traditional desktop computer, the setup of a Raspberry Pi device out of the box is always the same. There are specific steps and specific things that need to take place in a specific order to ensure the Pi device is setup correctly before it can be used. Contrary to all computer towers and personal laptops, there is some bottom-up setup that is required before you can use whatever operating system you choose to install on your Raspberry Pi, but as you will soon discover, it's not as difficult as it sounds.

Chapter 3: Setting It Up Out of the Box

Eben Upton, the imagination behind the Raspberry Pi, came up with the idea in 2006 after himself and his colleagues were frustrated by the dwindling number of students at their college, University of Cambridge. They were in the computer laboratory investigating why in the world students entering the program had such poor skill levels, and they wanted to do something about it. The incoming students usually had web design experience, but programming experience was starting to become very rare, which was a massive component of the program him and his colleagues were in at the time.

However, after doing some research, they found that the price of the sophisticated equipment necessary to teach these students these programming skills was far too expensive for beginning students to simply experiment with.

They found the cause was the quick advancement of family personal computers. Parents ended up moving to forbid the same types of experimentation on computers than were seen in prior decades, such as the 70s and 80s, because of the growing concerns of the internet as they surfaced. Plus, as these personal computers became easier to use, programming became more complicated and tinkering with the inner guts of a computer became far less necessary because of their growing efficiency.

This is where the idea for the Raspberry Pi came into play: Upton wanted to create a cheap and easily-programmable computer that could bring back this tinkering and experimental spirit that was found in earlier eras of computing. He wanted the device to be cheap enough so anyone of any knowledge base could tamper with it without running the risk of expensive mistakes they could not pay for. So, in 2006, Upton and his colleagues began working on the prototype for the Raspberry Pi. The Raspberry Pi Foundation was then established in 2009 as support for the device began to grow, and the first shipment of Raspberry Pis were then available by April 2012.

The device is so heavily wired into programming, in fact, that while the recommended programming language is Python, the Pi's system can handle dozens of different programming languages. Not only that, but the device can also run an infinite number of operating systems that a user can install onto the Pi device side-by-side in order to make those programming languages more compatible with the base system.

Now, when a user obtains their Raspberry Pi, there are different ways it can be setup out of the box. The easiest way is by using a program entitled NOOBS, which makes the out-of-box setup for the Raspberry Pi infinitely easier. If you are a beginner when it comes to programming, lines of code, and technology, then this will be the way you want to setup your device.

The great thing about this setup is that there is no requirement for fancy imaging software or programs, nor is there a need for network access. All you do is head to the Raspberry Pi Foundation's official website page, navigate to their downloads, and grab a copy of the NOOBS zip file. Then, you unzip the file onto a freshly formatted 4GB SD card. Then, when you boot up for the first time, it will prompt you to install one of several operating systems into the free space that exists on the card. This means you can either boot your Pi device with a "regular" operating system such as Raspbian, or you can boot it up with a specified operating system, like RaspBMC, which is a media-center operating system.

Here are the steps you need to take in order to boot up your Pi device out of the box using NOOBS:

- For the easiest route, purchase an SD card that comes preinstalled with NOOBS from any recognized Raspberry Pi distributor.

- For the Raspberry Pi Zero, Raspberry Pi 2, Raspberry Pi 3, A+, and B+ you will need a microSD card. For all other versions you will need a full-size SD card.

14

- If you choose to purchase your own 4GB SD card (though 8GB is recommended), this is what you do:

  - Use a personal computer that has an SD card reader and visit the "Downloads" page on the Raspberry Pi Foundation website.

  - Click on the file entitled "NOOBS", then click on "Download ZIP." This button will be under "NOOBS (offline and network install)."

  - Select the folder you want to save it to (hint hint: it's your SD card).

  - Unzip the file onto the SD card.

- If you run into issues with putting the unzipped file onto your SD card, then it might need to be formatted. Here is what you do if you need to format your SD card:

  - Go to the SD Association's website and download the SD Formatter 4.0 for either Windows or Mac, depending on which computer you are using.

  - Follow the instructions they prompt you in order to install the software onto your personal computer.

- Put your SD card into the computer or laptop's card reader. Make sure you take a look at the drive letter that has been assigned to your SD card, because that will be necessary later.

- Then, open up the SD formatter and select the drive letter that has been assigned to your SD card and format it accordingly.

- Now, once your card has been formatted (or once you have NOOBS unzipped onto your SD card):

- Drag and drop the files onto your SD card if they do not already appear and wait for the transfer process to complete.

- When the process has finished, take precautions to remove the SD card from your personal computer or laptop SD card reader and insert it into the SD card reader on your Raspberry Pi.

- Now you are ready for your first boot up!

- Plug in your mouse, monitor cables, and keyboard first.

- Now, plug the USB power cable into your Raspberry Pi device.

- Once you plug that power source into an outlet, the Pi device will turn on and a window will automatically appear. It will have a list of various operating systems you can install, and the recommendation for beginners is Raspbian.

- Check the box next to "Raspbian" and then click on "Install."

- The installation process for Raspbian will begin, and this will take awhile.

- When the installation is complete, your Pi device's configuration menu (raspi-config) will load and open. This is where you can set the date and time for the region you live in, turn on a Raspberry Pi camera board, and even create the users that will be utilizing the device.

- To exit this this menu, press the "Tab" button on your keyboard until it toggles over to "Finish," and then press "Enter."

- If it prompts you to login before you have created your own username and password:

  - The default login for Raspbian is the username "pi" without the quotes and password is "raspberry" without the quotes. Understand that you will not see anything pop up onto the screen when you begin typing the password.

This is just a general security feature, so don't let it startle you.

- Should you want to load the graphical user interface, simply type "startx" without the quotes and then press "Enter."

That is not the only way, however, to boot up your Raspberry Pi device out of the box.

This is how to install your Pi's operating system image onto an SD card using different imaging software than the one previously mentioned. If you are more in tune with technology and formatting and want to install a particular image rather than a general file, then this boot up guide is for you.

In order to download the image:

- It is recommended to use at least an 8GB SD card for writing these types of images. If you are not using Etcher, you will have to unzip the downloads (.zip) in order to get to the image file (.img) in order to write it to your SD card.

- On a side note: the Raspbian with PIXEL image utilizes a ZIP64 format. In order to un-compress this archive, you have to have an unzipping tool that supports this format. If you are using Windows, the program 7-Zip is a good one. For Mac users, the program The Unarchiver is a decent one. If you are using Linux, the program Unzip is what you want.

- Just because you have unzipped the file onto your SD card does not mean the image is readable. You have to have an image writing tool in order to install the image you have simply downloaded.

- This is where a program called Etcher comes into play. It is compatible with Linux, Windows, and Mac operating

17

systems, and is the easiest option to use. You can also write the image directly from the .zip file without unzipping it, if that suits you.

- Download Etcher and install it.

- Open Etcher and select the raspberry Pi image or zip file that is located on the hard drive of your computer.

- Select the SD card you want to write the image to (we are assuming you have already inserted your SD card into the card reader of the personal computer you are using. If you have not, do that now).

- Review everything and then click "Flash!" in order to begin the process of writing the data onto the SD card.

- Once you have the image properly downloaded onto the SD card, take precautionary measures to eject it from your personal computer and insert it into your Raspberry Pi device.

- Plug in all your peripherals (keyboard, mouse, and monitor) to the Pi device.

- Plug in the power source onto the Raspberry Pi board, then plug it into an outlet in order to boot it up for the first time.

- Follow the onscreen prompts and menu in order to select and install the image you have chosen to download onto your Pi device.

Those are the two most popular ways to format and boot up the Raspberry Pi out of the box. This device is something the user builds from the ground-up and is one of the most customizable pieces of technology in the marketplace today. You can choose your operating system, and if you cannot decide on one, you can format your Raspberry Pi to house and handle toggling between multiple operating systems. You can download massive amounts of software onto it that help you with whatever in-home project you have taken on, and it automatically comes equipped with a safe landscape to learn and tinker with in its most popular coding language, Python.

Chapter 4: Coding for the Raspberry Pi

The Raspberry Pi was originally designed to promote and encourage the younger generations to learn how to code. The "Pi" in Raspberry Pi comes from a programming language entitled Python, so the very idea of computer science and programming is literally written into the name of the device itself. While it has been on the market a short time compared to other microcomputers, there are many different programming languages that have been adapted for the Raspberry Pi, and it is this plethora of languages that creates the vibrant ecosystem that is quickly ramping up around the Raspberry Pi device.

This type of support is great to have because it projects that a technological device such as this one will be around for quite a long time to come.

There are ten major coding languages that are used in over 80% of technology the world uses now, and these can all be experimented with on the Raspberry Pi. However, understand that it is not limited to just these ten: if a language can be successfully compiled for the ARMv6 chip that powers the bulk of the Raspberry Pi, then it can be utilized on the Raspberry Pi.

Scratch is the most popular one. It is an entry-level programming language that already comes standard with the Raspberry Pi distribution and housed within the operating system, Raspbian. The reason why it is so popular, especially with young people, is because it was made specifically to target helping young people learn the basics of coding.

Python is next, and it is one of the primary programming languages that is hosted on Raspberry Pi. Fun fact: Python is actually named after Monty Python's Flying Circus, and references to the comedy show are regularly encouraged when someone is creating an example and/or teaching documentation to help those learn the coding language. This is a program that comes not only equipped on the Raspberry Pi, but it comes with its own terminal screen built into the main operating system menu.

HTML5 is next on the list, and this is a mark-up language that makes the entire internet tick. It was created by Tim Berners-Lee while he was working at CERN in Geneva, and it was supposed to be a way to allow scientists within the organization to share their documents with one another on a closed network. However, it eventually went global and has turned into the internet as we know it today. HTML stands tall and proud as the primary building block of the internet: it tells each browser how to layout a web page, it lets one website link out to another, and it even instructs website designers on how to build a basic website. With this newest upgrade to HTML, which is the one we are talking about currently, it has made embedding audio clips and videos into applications and web pages easier and not as taxing on a smartphone or tablet if they navigate to the page and wish to play the excerpt.

JavaScript is a language many people are familiar with but not many people understand how to work. This is a scripting language that pairs alongside HTML in order to add specific facets of interactive natures to websites. JavaScript was invented, and is currently maintained by, the World Wide Web Consortium, and it is this same group that looks after CSS and HTML to make sure everything fits perfectly into the puzzle they are wishing to create. JavaScript also adds client-side scripting to web browsers, which simply means an individual can create drop down menus, do calculations, and a million other things at the drop of a hat.

And, as if that was not enough, JavaScript also helps companies like Google and Yahoo to improve their online Maps and how those maps can be used.

JQUERY is the most popular JavaScript library. It can run on any browser you wish and it makes scripting HTML much simpler. With this particular programming language, you are able to create rich interfaces of websites as well as rich interactive components while having a very small amount of knowledge when it comes to using JavaScript.

Java is another main language, but do not confuse this with JavaScript. When Java hit the scene, it was greeted with open arms by many developers because it was the first programming language where a programmer or coder could write a specific program that ran on any operating system, whether it was a Windows machine or Unix box, without having to completely rewrite the code. This incredible leap forward changed the entire face of the coding industry because developers no longer had to write in different languages for each operating system they might use. They also no longer had to rewrite code simply because they were compiling different iterations for every computer they wanted to run their specific code on. Using Java meant they could simplify the code once and then make it run anywhere they stuck it.

C Programming Language was written by Dennis Ritchie utilizing the B language as its model. C is one of the most widely used languages in the world today and it is used in absolutely everything from building complete operating systems, to providing a foundation for simple programming languages. For example, Linux is the operating system that runs the basis of Raspbian for Raspberry Pi, and this is largely written in C Programming Language. The design for this particular coding language influenced many other coding languages, including many of the ones we have already mentioned in this chapter. Not only that, it also helped design the programming language Objective C, which is what Apple uses to create applications for iPhones and iPads.

C++ was developed by a Danish developer as a way to enhance C Programming Language. This particular coding language is used in a million different areas and circumstances that include embedded software, graphical applications, and hardware design. Not only that, but many people utilize it to program video games. C++ was created specifically to add on object-oriented features to the C Programming Language, and it has been embraced graciously ever since.

Perl is another language we are discussing in this chapter, and it has regularly been called the "duct tape" that "holds" the internet together. Some people even call it the "Swiss Army chainsaw" of scripting languages. These names are given to it because this coding language has incredible flexibility and adaptability in its world. Before Perl arrived on the scene, the internet was simply a collection of static pages that provided information. Perl was what added that dynamic element we are so used to seeing today on the internet, which meant that for the first time websites could be put together at the drop of a hat. Among a slew of other things, it also enabled sites that base themselves off e-commerce, such as eBay and Amazon, to come into being. It made sites like that possible.

The last one on this list is Erlang, but do not think that is because it is last it is the least important. Erlang is a programming language that is used by developers when there is absolutely no room for failure. If you are running a nuclear power plant or designing a new air traffic control system, this means that all those mission-critical situations where a breakdown in computing can be disastrous requires something that has little to no room for technological failure. Erlang can create programs that run across several different computers and can help with this issue: it is designed so that if one particular computer fails, the others can then make up for that failure, which means the system never really goes down.

If you want to teach yourself code, or if your child is expressing interest in learning how to write code, then the Raspberry Pi is the perfect device for you. However, once someone obtains a Raspberry Pi it can be difficult to figure out where to go from there. The first thing you need to look into is something called Raspberry Jams. These are meetups that are community-lead that center around people getting together who want to learn and teach about the Raspberry Pi and all of its facets. Raspberry Jams are growing in popularity, especially in bigger cities, because many technological event meet-ups are usually geared towards adults.

Raspberry Jams are geared towards individuals of all ages. The only requirement is that you come to either learn or teach coding and everything it has to do with the Raspberry Pi.

The best thing you can do for any beginner who is learning how to code with the Raspberry Pi is to begin with Scratch.

While you will never get a coding job writing in Scratch for living, that is not the point. The point of scratch is to take the code and turn it into something beautiful and visual. This makes it less intimidating for beginners and the animations at the end make them more prone to "play" the game.

Then, the next step up from Scratch is Python. This is a simple educational programming language you can use on your career resume of programming abilities. Python was designed specifically to be easy to read and simple to write. It has its own interpreter that comes on the Raspberry Pi device, which is the thing that actually runs the code once you write it, and the programming environment on the Pi device comes with strict rules that are enforced to help individuals learning Python write clean, good code.

Another way you can play around with code that makes it easy to learn is playing with Minecraft Pi. If you are not familiar with Minecraft, it is essentially a digital Lego game. Just as you would take Legos and construct a pretend spaceship, a pretend person, or a pretend castle with plastic bricks, you take all of these elements and put them onto a computer screen and you work with virtual bricks to build objects, houses, animals, and the world you want to see. The great thing about Minecraft, and what makes it so popular with children, is the fact that there are no hard limits as to what you can build in it. Your creations that you come up with can be as big or small as you want and they can be as simple or as ambitious as the imagination allows. It is an unadulterated experience where children can truly flex the whole of their imagination without ever getting themselves into trouble, and there is a version of this game for the Raspberry Pi device that can be downloaded that incorporates this world with the foundations of coding. It is free of charge and it is designed to run on the limited hardware of the Raspberry Pi. This made a legitimate video game a vehicle to teach programming because of the way it is setup: you use Python as a way to maneuver the bricks and components within the game in order to set them up, so not only is the user building their own world, they are learning and reinforcing the rules of the Python programming language.

Programming and learning coding languages on the Raspberry Pi is what the device was originally built for, so it only stands to reason that this would be one of the biggest and easiest facets to utilize. However, over time other people have come up with other uses the Raspberry Pi has outside of simply learning and teaching coding languages, and it has made the Pi device the most customizable technological piece of equipment on the market.

It has also given way to some of the coolest in-home projects anyone could ever take on.

Chapter 5: Different Uses of the Raspberry Pi

One of the great things about the Raspberry Pi is that many individuals have come up with varying projects that can be constructed with this device. Yes, it is a powerful tool for teaching varying programming techniques, but it is also a versatile piece of equipment that can serve as the heart of many different projects.

One of the fun things you can do is modify your Pi device. There are many Raspberry Pi kits that come with colorful cases in all shades of the rainbow, and they utilize the art of injection molding in order to get the exact shape of the Pi device you currently have. It is a fun way to customize the look of your Raspberry Pi without destroying the integrity of it.

You can also make your own Pi case. If that is a project you wish to take on, there are many kits sold on the open market that allow you to piece together your own, fully-customizable template that you can either cut up and glue together, or trace onto your own materials in order to assemble yourself. As if the Raspberry Pi was not customizable enough, this is thrown into the mix, and it allows you to showcase who you are through this valuable piece of technology.

You can also use your Pi device as a living room personal computer. Now that you have your Pi device in a cool looking case, utilize the HDMI ports and the input/output hookups in order to hook your television monitor up to your device. This turns your television into the Raspberry Pi's main monitor, meaning you have whatever kind of television you desire pumping out the visual sourcing of your internet. Ever wondered what it would be like to code on a 55" HD-TV screen?

Well, now you can figure it out.

And while your Raspberry Pi is hooked up to the television screen, go ahead and open your internet browser! Not only is it now your very own personal computer, it is also a gigantic web browser.

You can also take your Pi device down a more retro road. You can set up your pie device to emulate just about any old video game consoles, from Mega Drive to SNES. It is not a quick install and is better done on the newer generations of the Raspberry Pi, but it is not impossible on the older generations if that is what you are utilizing.

And do not worry, this is not only free, but it is legal.

But, if you really want to go retro and enjoy massive do-it-yourself projects, then consider going arcade with your Raspberry Pi. The wonderful thing about the Raspberry Pi is that it can be the guts for something. Many people have purchased kits off the internet that send them the parts to create their own laptop computer, desktop computer, camera, home surveillance system, and touchscreen tablet, all while using the Raspberry Pi as the main innards. But, you can take this really cool idea one step further by using it as the innards for a full-sized retro arcade game. If you can get your hands on a full-sized arcade cabinet, then you can take on making your very own, stand alone, full-sized retro arcade game. Complete with the joystick!

And, while the subject of retro is still in our sights, you can also run incredibly retro and outdated operating systems on your Pi device, such as Windows 3.0. If you want to run Windows 3.0, then follow these instructions:

- Go to Kirsle and navigate to the VirtualBox (VDI) image

- Extract it and convert it to a raw image that you can use by opening a terminal command window and typing: vboxmanage clonehd "image.vdi" "image.img" --format RAW

- Side note: make sure you replace both "image" slots with the name of the image you are toggling.

- Then, you have to install the QEMU. Do this by typing in sudo apt-get install qemu

- Then, you have to convert this raw image by typing in qemu- img convert -f raw image.img -O qcow2 image.qcow

- Then, you run all of this by finally typing in qemu. Image.qcow

This is not perfect, and does freeze up some, but many people have stated that it is a fun little throwback, even if you choose not to use it regularly.

Many fun uses of the Raspberry Pi also stem from the world of robotics. This was the arena that took off in terms of utilizing the Raspberry Pi when it first came onto the market, and they are the community that gave the type of criticism and feedback that prompted several more generations of the Pi device in order to get it to where it is currently. However, even if you are not familiar with robotics, there are many tutorials out there on what parts you need to purchase and where you need to purchase them in order to make your own robotic arm that you can control and power with your very own Pi device.

Not only that, but there are many beginner robotics kits out there that will ship you all of the things you need to make your very own robot. It is rudimentary, so it is perfect for those just learning about robotics, and it is yet another way the Raspberry Pi has been turned into a teaching tool for the future of technology.

If you want to take on something a little goofier, then try the tutorial that can be found anywhere online that walks you through how to make a functioning Raspberry Pi keyboard solely out of beer cans!

That's right. Beer cans. As in, you touch the top of the beer can and it types the letter, number, or character that is associated with the beer can you just pressed.

You can also utilize the Raspberry Pi to make your very own secure cloud server! By using OwnCloud, you can transform your Pi device into your very own cloud storage container that is not only secured from the outside world, but can be tailored so that only you can access it.

No more paying for extra cloud storage!

One of the most frequent projects to come out of using the Raspberry Pi is an RPi UAV. If you do not know what that is, then you will know this phrasing: flying a drone. There are various tutorials popping up everywhere that are now showing people how to make, put together, and fly their own Raspberry Pi-powered drones! It is a project for someone who is more familiar with robotics than the average beginner, but it is a project that is definitely worth working your way towards in terms of your skill level.

You can also create your own weather station. If you are a weather guru like many individuals, then you can use some tutorials found on the Raspberry Pi Foundation website to make your very own predictive weather station! Not only that, but the device you create can also backlog data, just in case you need last month's weather stats for any reason.

The Raspberry Pi can also be used for home automation. Gone are the days where you have to pay millions of dollars for a smart home, because the Raspberry Pi makes something like that possible on a budget. There is a product entitled PiFace that is perfect for this type of project, and what it does is it hooks up your Pi device and enables it to detect specific switch states from whatever door sensor you hook it up to. You can also hook it up to pressure pads, swipe devices, or any other type of "automatic" sensor you wish, making it the most customizable home automation project on the market.

You can also purchase multiple Raspberry Pi's and hook them up together, utilizing their GPIO pins. What does this do? Well, it increases memory, computing and processing power, and enhances the graphic state of the image projected onto whatever monitor you are using.

Simply put, you can make your very own supercomputer.

If none of the above options interest you, then this might: the Raspberry Pi can also be turned into its very own media center. For some people, putting in the money to build their own media center is just not worth it. The sheer amount of storage it requires along with all the hookups and the purchasing of material to store is a hassle, and many never take on the project. But, with the Raspberry Pi, turning it into its own media center is as easy as downloading the specific application you wish to use and customizing it from within.

For some, they enjoy making their own eBook library. The Raspberry Pi can hold an exorbitant amount of eBooks, and it can even store audiobooks that can be listened to simply by running the book, plugging in headphones into the 3.5mm phone jack, and sitting back. However, you can also flip through the pages of a book in your organized and image-heavy eBook library on whatever monitor you decide to hook up to your device.

55″ books, anyone?

Not only that, but the Raspberry Pi can be set up to play different types of media. From storing movies in a library to saving images that can be played in succession, and in time, to music you are also storing in your media center, the Raspberry Pi can be turned into an all-in-one media storage for anything and everything you could ever want. It takes a bit of time to tweak, and if you have a massive library you might want to consider purchasing another Pi device and hooking the two up via their GPIO pins, but many people have taken this route and said it is the single greatest thing they ever did with their Pi device.

Another small use that can be taken on by the Raspberry Pi is a wireless internet booster. For many people who live in larger or oddly-designed homes, sometimes there can be dead spots when it comes to where wireless internet will and will not reach. You can take a Raspberry Pi device and better configure it in order to enhance and extend the range of your wireless network. If you have that one room at the back of the house that only gets one tick of wireless internet, you can tweak it so that it will have full-strength Wi-Fi!

Also, you can make it so you sit on your own porch or sunbathe in your own backyard while still picking up a strong internet signal. Just make sure to take the necessary security precautions you can on your Pi device when it comes to locking down who can and cannot use your wireless internet.

When it comes to the world of projects, the Raspberry Pi delivers. Believe it or not, this is only scratching the surface of all the things individuals have found the Pi device to be capable of, and many more projects (like the drone-flying) are being created and discovered every single day!

But, it gets better: if you enjoyed these projects, and if any sparked your interest, then read on into the next chapter to find outlines of projects you can take on by yourself!

Chapter 6: Raspberry Pi Projects

To get you started, we have provided two step-by-step projects that are readily accessible for the Raspberry Pi! The guides will outline what you need to do, what you need to have, and which Raspberry Pi device would be best for the project.

The first project outline is for creating your own wireless network printer! This project is perfect for people who do not have the ability to purchase the fancy printers that are created nowadays. It can be used with any old school printer you find in an old office, thrift shop, or even in an attic somewhere.

Here is what you will need:

- Wireless internet connection
- Printer
- Raspberry Pi 3 (or any other Raspberry Pi generation that has both a USB port and wireless internet capabilities)
- USB Printer (if the printer you are using does not have a USB port, then you need to get a parallel-to-USB adaptor)
- USB cable that runs from your printer to your Raspberry Pi device

The tutorial we are giving is going to be based off your Raspberry Pi device running Raspbian. Now, two things you have to do before we begin this project: you have to update and upgrade your Raspberry Pi.

- To update and upgrade the device, pull up a terminal command window.
- To update, enter in sudo apt-get update
- Hit enter to run the command, and then enter sudo apt-get upgrade
- Hit enter to run the command, and you are finished!

Now, with everything connected and setup (your Raspberry Pi device needs to be hooked up via a USB port to your printer, and your Raspberry Pi needs to be hooked up to your wireless internet), you have to make sure your USB printer is being detected.

- Open a command line within a new terminal window and enter lsusb
- This should bring up a list of USB devices that are connected to your Raspberry Pi. Check to make sure your printer is one of them.

After seeing your printer there, the next step is to install Samba.
- Enter the command line sudo apt-get install samba
- Press enter to run and follow any prompted instructions to install the program.

Now, you need to install CUPS, which is the Common Unix Printing System. Understand that Samba has to be installed first, so wait until it is done downloading and doing its thing before you do this step.
- In a new command line, enter sudo apt-get install cups
- Hit enter to run the command line and wait for it to install. This program is what will provide the necessary drivers for your printer.

Now, you need to add a default user to the printer administration group so you can have access to it from your Pi device.
- To do this, enter sudo usermod −a −G lpadmin pi into a new command line.
- Hit enter to run the command.

Now, it is time to setup your printer with your Raspberry Pi device. All of the things done before were only preparing your Pi device to be setup with your printer. So, here is how you begin this process:

- Open a fresh terminal window and type in sudo rasp-config
- Scroll down to the option that says "boot_behavior" and hit "enter" on your keyboard.
- This pulls up the GUI interface

- Navigate (with the terminal window still open in the background) to your browser and start it up.
- Type in 127.0.0.1:631 and hit "enter" on your keyboard.
- When the screen is done loading, choose the "Administration tab."
- Once you have clicked this tab, there should be some options, and one of those options should be "Add new printer." Click it.
- When prompted, enter in your Raspbian credentials and choose your printer from the provided list.
- Go to the next screen and follow the command prompts as necessary.
- Eventually, it will ask you to confirm your details. Take the time to make sure everything is correct. At this point, if you wish, you can assign your printer an easier name so you can identify it faster.
- After you have looked over all the information, select "Share This Printer," then click "continue."

Now, this next page might take a while to load, so do not let that startle you. The Raspberry Pi is communicating with the printer at rapid speeds and transmitting quite a lot of data. What is happening is the entire ecosystem of device driver names is being uploaded. However, once this entire list has downloaded, you can select the correct printer once again (which should now be highlighted by default) and click "continue."

- After all of this, select "Add Printer," then select "Default Options."

Once this is all completed, your printer should be ready to start accepting jobs! If you want to run a test print, then navigate back to the main window that houses your printer's options, select "Maintenance," and then select "Print Test Page."

Now, once you have the two devices connected, you need to make sure you have access to the Raspberry Pi from your Windows (or whatever other browsing option you prefer). In order to do this, it requires editing the Samba configuration file in /etc/samba/smb.conf. Find your way to this configuration file and type in everything as follows:

```
# CUPS printing.  See also the cupsaddsmb(8) manpage in the
# cupsys-client package.
printing = cups
printcap name = cups
[printers]
comment = All Printers
browseable = no
path = /var/spool/samba
printable = yes
guest ok = yes
read only = yes
create mask = 0700
# Windows clients look for this share name as a source of
downloadable
# printer drivers
[print$]
comment = Printer Drivers
path = /usr/share/cups/drivers
browseable = yes
read only = yes
guest ok = no
```

After all of this is entered in, hold down your CTRL and press "W" in order to search for the "workgroup" function.
```
workgroup = your_workgroup_name
wins support = yes
```
Make sure you replace "your_workgroup_name" with whatever workgroup name you choose. Then, save everything, exit the GUI, and navigate to the terminal window so you can restart Samba.

- Type in sudo /etc/init.d/samba restart
- Hit enter to restart the program!

Once Samba restarts itself, you can then switch to your Windows personal computer and add a new printer. First, check to make sure your Pi device is visible to the computer itself.

- Open your browser, pull up the main menu, and click on the "Network" tab.
- Go to "Control Panel," then click "Hardware and Sound," then click "Devices and Printers," then choose "Advanced Printer Setup."
- At this point, the system will scan for devices.
- If you have set this up with a Mac computer, you can add a new printer in the way you usually would.
- If you need to open up the administration for the CUPS printer on your network computer, type in http://[RPI.IP.ADDRESS.HERE]:631

Of course, replace "RIP.IP.ADDRESS.HERE" with whatever IP address your Raspberry Pi currently has.
Voila! You have set up a connection between your old printer and the Raspberry Pi which now siphons off internet access to the old printer so you can print wirelessly from that printer from your desktop computer!

The next project we are taking on is a bit simpler, but it's really awesome. The next step-by-step project is going to show you how to turn your Raspberry Pi into its very own media center! Here is what you will need:

- Your Pi device (the Raspberry Pi 2 is the best for this project, but any latest generation will do!)
- Either a composite video cable or an HDMI cable
- A Class 10 8GB SD card (make sure both your Pi device and the computer you will be using to help with the project both have card readers on them)
- USB-based peripherals (keyboard, mouse, etc.)
- An Ethernet cable
- Your microSD power supply cable to power your Pi device
- A remote control (if you do not want to use your keyboard and mouse to control the media center once it is up and running)

- A USB hard drive (this is only necessary if you do not want to stream your videos from other computers inputted into the Raspberry Pi)
- An outside case for your Pi device (this is only necessary if you do not want the bare bones of your finished project sitting out)
- 3.5mm stereo audio cable (this is only necessary if you are using some sort of analog video input and you want to connect a set of external speakers to your Raspberry Pi. If you are using an HDMI input, then this is automatically null and void)
- The OSMC installer (this will put Raspbmc onto your SD card)

Before we begin this project, let's do a little rundown of what you will and will not get with this media center. You will get:

- A media center that can play 720p videos perfectly.
- A silent media center that does not compete with the sound of your movie.
- A media center that can play images in succession on whatever monitor screen you choose.
- The ability to store and stream movies.

Here is what you will not get:

- The ability to stream content (like access to your Hulu and Netflix accounts).
- You might experience some stuttering with 1080p videos.
- This depends, however. If you play them over the network, they probably will stutter. If you have them stored onto a USB hard drive, they might not.

Now, here are the steps you need to take in order to create your own media center:

- Put Raspbmc onto your SD card.

- To do this, insert your SD card into your alternative computer.Use the correct installer in order to download the program and run it on your computer so you can obtain Raspbmc to put onto your SD card.

- Once it is successfully downloaded to your SD card, properly eject it.

- Now, you need to hook up your Pi device in order to install Raspbmc.

- Plug in the HDMI cable into your television from your Pi device.

- Plug the Ethernet cable into your router from your Pi device.

- Insert the SD card into your Pi device.

- Plug in the micro USB power cable into your wall from your Pi device.

- Once it boots up, it should automatically begin the installation process from the SD card.

- This might take a while, so go get yourself a sandwich, and once it is done installing, it should automatically reboot and open with Raspbmc.

- Now, it is time to tweak your settings for optimal playback experiences!

- Navigate to "Settings," then choose "System," then choose "Video Output." You are going to be watching 720p videos, then toggle the setting to "720p."

- From "Video Output," navigate to "Video Calibration." If you find that the interface stretches beyond the boundaries of your monitor, then this is where you will toggle those boundaries in order to get the screen to fit. Use the wizard housed within this component to automatically gauge and set it for you!

- Navigate out and go to "Programs," then select "Raspbmc Settings," then click "System Configuration." This is where you will be able to allow the Pi device to overclock while in media center mode, which will help everything run a bit faster. Try the "Fast" setting first.

There you have it! Your very own media center courtesy of your Raspberry Pi. Now, all you need to do is pull up any tutorials you might need on how to add videos, images, and music to your library. You can also find ways to install add-ons to boost your experience, and you can find other ways to customize the interface in order to suit your needs.

When it comes to your Raspberry Pi device, these are just two of the many popular projects ranging from beginner to expert. Choose one of these to begin with and familiarize yourself with how the Raspberry Pi is setup to take on projects, and build your ecosystem from there!
After all, the only thing holding you back is your own imagination.

Conclusion

Thanks again for taking the time to read this book!

You should now have a good understanding of Raspberry Pi, and be ready to get started!

If you enjoyed this book, please take the time to leave me a review on Amazon. I appreciate your honest feedback, and it really helps me to continue producing high quality books.

www.ingramcontent.com/pod-product-compliance
Lightning Source LLC
Chambersburg PA
CBHW060931050326
40689CB00013B/3051